Winning Starts With Beginning

Robert H. Schuller

Thomas Nelson Publishers
Nashville • Camden • New York

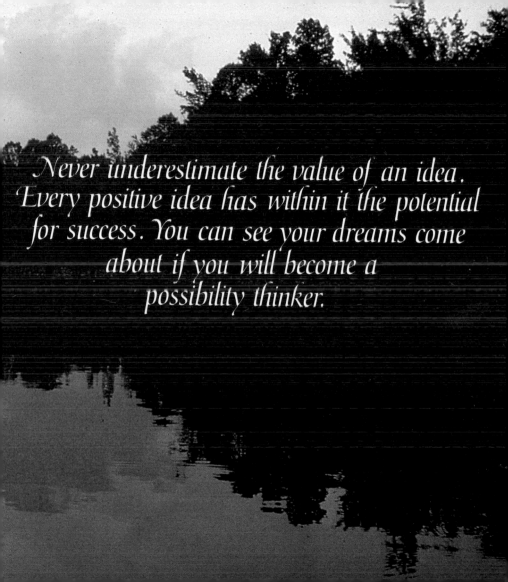

Never underestimate the value of an idea. Every positive idea has within it the potential for success. You can see your dreams come about if you will become a possibility thinker.

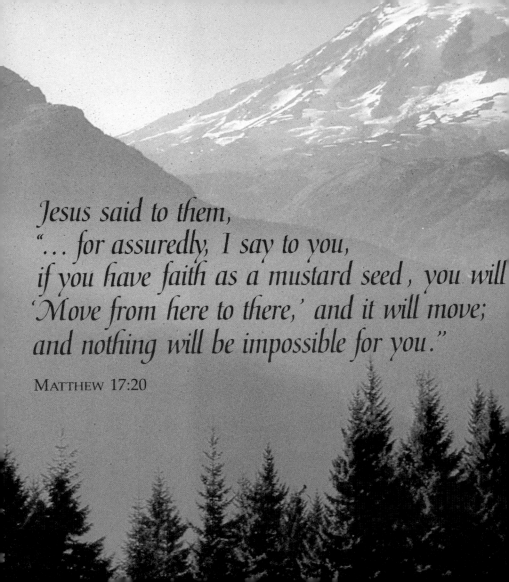

Jesus said to them,
"... for assuredly, I say to you,
if you have faith as a mustard seed, you will
'Move from here to there,' and it will move;
and nothing will be impossible for you."

MATTHEW 17:20

say to this mountain,

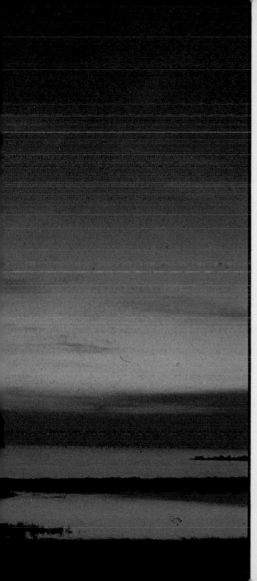

Possibility Thinking in Action

*I*n July 1980, Judy Hall, mother of two teen age daughters, found herself unemployed. Divorced and without steady income, Judy wondered how she would possibly survive.

She easily could have gotten discouraged, but she didn't. She scraped together enough dollars to pack up herself and her two daughters and return to the state of their birth— Hawaii.

After returning to Hawaii, she wanted the comfort of a muumuu, the loose-fitting dress of the Islands, but also a garment with enough style to be worn to non-Hawaiian events. As she shopped for such a muumuu, she discovered that all of them were sold in one size, and all had a similar Hawaiian print.

She suddenly remembered that the secret of success is to find a need and fill it. She purchased some fabric in a "mainland" print and proceeded to make for herself a muumuu with a decorative border at the hem. She customized the fit so that it was comfortable but not so loose-fitting as to lose all sense of line and design. The final result was something very distinctive.

Beyond a doubt, this was a totally new concept in manufacture and design of muumuus. Judy remembered that one can test an idea to see if it will be successful by asking four questions.

• Is it practical, and will it fill a vital human need? A muumuu is exceptionally practical because it fits any lady, of any shape.

• Can it be done beautifully? Yes, a muumuu can be made with more sophisticated draping and tapering and with a layered look like formal dresses on the mainland.

• Can it be done differently enough so that it will stand out from all the others? Judy decided that it could if she didn't use Hawaiian prints.

• Can it receive the stamp of excellence and be a little better than anything else that is being offered? Yes! With one hundred dollars and this confidence she decided to start.

"Dr. Schuller," Judy Hall told me recently, "I made my first muumuu ten months ago. Today I'm turning out 123 dresses a month!

"When my friends saw me with my two children and no income, they really worried about how we were going to survive. When I told them I was going to go into the dress-making business, with my own brand and design of muumuus, they laughed at me. They said, 'You're going to try to sell muumuus to Hawaiians? Why don't you go to Alaska and sell snow to the Eskimos?'

"Those were the kinds of comments I heard, but guess what?" she said enthusiastically. "I just received an order to make all of the muumuus for the two hundred girls in the graduating class of one of the largest high schools in Honolulu."

A single, divorced mother of two children, with no money and no special training, was able to invade a surplus market with a new product and develop a super successful enterprise.

It works! Believe me! Possibility thinking works!

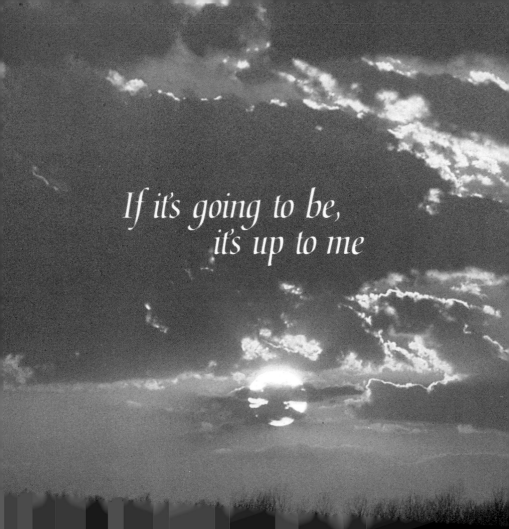

If it's going to be,
it's up to me

*N*obody is more guilty of locked-in thinking than trained, educated professionals. They have been so disciplined, so trained that as they develop a discipline, an expertise, they also develop locked-in thinking.

The elevator at the El Cortez Hotel in San Diego couldn't handle the

The Value of an Idea

traffic. The experts—engineers and architects—were called in. They concluded that they could put another elevator in by cutting a hole in each floor and installing the motor for the new elevator in the basement. The plans were drawn up. Everything was in order. The architect and the engineer came into the lobby discussing it. The janitor, who was there with his mop, heard them say they were going to chop holes in the floors.

The janitor said, "That's going to make a mess."

The engineer said, "Of course. But we'll get help for you, don't worry."

The janitor replied, "You'll have to close the hotel for a while."

"Well, if we have to close the hotel for a while, we'll close the hotel. We can't possibly survive without another elevator."

The janitor said, "Do you know what I would do if I were you?"

The architect arrogantly asked, "What?"

"I'd build the elevator on the outside."

The architect and the engineer just looked at each other.

They built the elevator on the outside—the first time in the history of architecture that an elevator was built on the outside of a building.

Better to do something imperfectly
than to do nothing flawlessly

Ten
Commandments
of Possibility
Thinking

$\mathscr{N}$ever underestimate the value of an idea. Every positive idea has within it the potential for success if it is managed properly. How do we manage ideas so effectively that we can be assured of success? Through the Ten Commandments of Possibility Thinking—that's how! If you obey these commandments for possibility thinking, you will be amazed at the success you will achieve.

1. Never reject a possibility because you see something wrong with it!

There is something wrong with every good idea. It's amazing how people sit in a deliberating meeting and respond to an opportunity only by finding fault with it. Don't throw away a suggestion when you see a problem. Instead, isolate the negative from the possibility.

2. Never reject a possibility because you won't get the credit!

Don't worry about getting the credit. If you do, you'll become ego-involved in decision-making. Decisions must never be based on ego needs.

They must be based on human needs and market pressures that transcend your own desires. God can do tremendous things through the person who doesn't care who gets the credit.

3. Never reject an idea because it's impossible!

Almost every great idea is impossible when it is first born. The greatest ideas today are yet impossible! Possibility thinkers take great ideas and turn the impossibilities into possibilities. That's progress!

4. Never reject a possibility because your mind is already made up!

I've had to change my mind publicly more than once. People who never change their minds are either perfect or stubborn. I'm not perfect and neither are you. I'd rather change plans while still in port, than to set sail and sink at sea.

5. Never reject an idea because it's illegal!

Listen carefully, or you'll misinterpret this commandment. Some of the greatest ideas are

impossible because they are illegal today. You should never violate the law, but don't reject an idea because it's illegal. You might be able to get the law changed!

6. Never reject an idea because you don't have the money, manpower, muscle, or months to achieve it!

If you don't have them, you can get them.

Spend enough time, use enough energy, develop enough human resources, acquire enough financial capital, and you can do almost anything. Don't reject an idea just because you don't have the necessary power. Make the commitment to do what's great, then solve the problems.

7. *Never reject an idea because it will create conflict!*

The longer I've studied possibility thinking, the more I've come to one conclusion. You can never develop a possibility without creating problems. Every idea worth anything is bound to be rejected by someone.

8. *Never reject an idea because it's not your way of doing things!*

Learn to accommodate. Prepare to compromise. A different style, a new policy, a change in tradition—all are opportunities to grow.

9. *Never reject an idea because it might fail!*

Every idea worth anything has failure potential within it. You never reject an idea because there's some risk involved. You isolate the risk, insulate it, and eventually eliminate it.

10. *Never reject an idea because it's sure to succeed!*

There are people today who back off if they are sure they will succeed. One reason is that these persons begin to imagine the ego fulfillment this success would give, and with an excuse of being humble, they pull out. Just because an idea is going to be a success, don't be against it.

The Ten Commandments for Possibility Thinkers—where do I get them? All ten come from the Bible. All ten come from Jesus Christ—the World's Greatest Possibility Thinker. He said, "If you have faith as a mustard seed, you will say to this mountain, 'Move from here to there,' and it will move; and nothing will be impossible for you" (Matt. 17:20).

Open your mind to God.
Ideas will flow in. One of these will be the

idea that God means for you to grab hold of.

Adapting an Idea

I have a dear friend who, like many others, was caught in the depression of the thirties. He was broke, penniless. He couldn't control his poverty, but he didn't surrender to the forces of the depression.

He was a salesman and not doing too well. One night, one of his fellow salesmen said, "Hey, did you hear about the guy who made so much money with Coca-Cola? You know, it used to be that the only way you could get a glass of soda was from a soda fountain. But then this guy came up with a way to bottle it. He told the Coca-Cola company that they could use his idea if they would give him a fraction of 1 percent of their increased sales. That minute percentage made him a millionaire."

That day my friend had been to the gas station because he needed oil in his car. In those days, the only way you could get oil was to go to a gas station where they pumped it out of huge drums and poured it into your car. Later that night he thought to himself, "I wonder if I could bottle oil?" Then he thought, "No, if the bottle broke, there would be a mess. But cans would work!"

So he went to a can company and said, "Can you sell me cans?" He went to a friend who owned a Pennsylvania oil well that produced so much oil he couldn't market it.

Then he went to a grocery chain and said, "I've got an idea how you can vastly increase your retail sales. I'll tell you how if you'll give me just seventy-five dollars for every freight car load of oil you sell."

They said, "O.K., what's your idea?"

"Sell automobile oil in cans. I'll provide them to you."

"Canned car oil?"

"Yes."

At only seventy-five dollars per freight car of cans, he became a multimillionaire during the Great Depression. He used it as the base of his now-enormous financial empire.

*Nobody is a total failure if
he dares to try to do
something worthwhile*

Dare to Decide

You handle ideas by making some kind of a decision. Winning starts with beginning! And to begin, you must do something *now.*

What do you do when you have a good idea? Just observe how differently people respond to ideas:

1. *Insecure people hibernate.* They run away from good ideas. They're afraid they might fail or that they might have to spend too much effort. And, like a bear that feels the first whisper of a winter wind and rushes off, tail between his legs, to hide out until the sun comes back months later, some people hibernate.

2. *Lazy people luxuriate*. They don't pay much attention to ideas. They want to enjoy the pleasures of this life. They'll get serious later on, probably when they're old. Maybe they'll even get religion.

3. *Wounded people commiserate*. They say, "Oh, it's a good idea, but I couldn't do it. I've tried it so often. I've tried to lose weight. I've tried all kinds of diets, but I keep getting fatter." Or, "I've tried to quit smoking twenty times in my life, and I've even torn up the package of cigarettes and thrown it in the wastebasket." Don't commiserate.

4. *Foolish people procrastinate*. They put off acting on their ideas. "Later on, when I'm ready, I'll do something about it." Don't wait until you're ready to make big decisions, or you'll never accomplish half of what you could. The difference between the high achiever and the low achiever is this: The high achiever almost always makes decisions before he's ready to move.

5. *Wise people dedicate*. They're do-it-now people. No grass grows under their feet. That's why they don't waste the most precious thing in the world—a good idea. They don't waste a good moment or a good opportunity.

How do you handle your good ideas? Don't hibernate. Don't luxuriate. Don't commiserate. Don't procrastinate. Dedicate yourself to that idea that has come from God. And then you can become the person you want to be!

How do you dedicate? How do you get started? Let me give you this clue: Don't wait for an inspiration. Use your head, and your heart will follow. Don't wait until you feel like it to make the move. If you wait until you feel like it, emotion will run you instead of reason.

Frequently I tackled an idea and said, "I'm going to do something about it," although I didn't feel like it. When I started writing this book, I did not feel like it! If I had waited until I got inspired, nothing would have happened. A published author will tell you how to write. Simply set a specific time to go to the typewriter and type. And you may not feel like it when you start, but pretty soon the inspiration comes.

You may need to go on a diet, but you don't feel like dieting. You're waiting until you feel like it. Don't! Discipline yourself for one full day, and then for two days, and do you know what? After two days you'll feel like it! Use your head, and your heart will follow!

I've learned another thing: I can do anything I think I can . . . but I can't do anything alone. I've taught this, preached it, written it, and tried it, and it's true. I always need someone to support me! Don't try to handle your dreams alone. It won't work.

Winning starts with beginning, and beginning starts with a single action.

Do something great with a great idea. Whatever it is that you should be doing—a concept for self-improvement, a dream, a goal, or a commitment to Jesus Christ—I want you to do it. Decide that this is going to be the day you're going to do something about it!

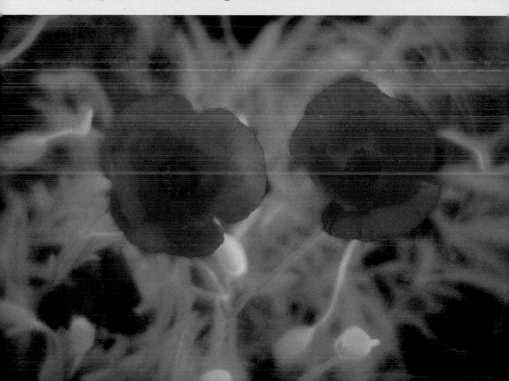

George Johnson

A good friend of mine, a black man named George Johnson, has experienced racism. He grew up in Chicago, polishing shoes in a barber shop. George used to hear his black friends say, "I wish I could straighten my hair."

One day while George was shining a man's shoes, he asked him, "What do you do?"

"I'm a chemist," the man replied.

"What do chemists do?" George asked.

"I mix things," the man explained.

"Do you think you could mix something that would straighten my hair?"

The chemist said, "Maybe I can put something together."

He did. George tried it on his hair, and it worked. He bottled the product and sold it to some of his friends and a few stores. Soon he built a sales force to sell "Ultra-Sheen." Today, George Johnson's personal fortune is over several million dollars. That's not bad for someone who was once a shoeshine boy.

How Do You Treat Ideas?

*W*hat kind of a person are you? Often we hear the question: How do you treat people? A far more important question is this: How do you treat ideas?

Treat ideas like newborn babies.
Treat them tenderly . . .
    They can get killed pretty quickly.
Treat them gently . . .
    They can be bruised in infancy.
Treat them respectfully . . .
    They can be the most valuable things
    that ever come into your life.
Treat them protectively . . .
    Don't let them get away.
Treat them nutritionally . . .
    Feed them, and feed them well.
Treat them antiseptically . . .
    Don't let them get infected with the germs
    of negative thoughts.
Treat them responsibly!
    Respond! Act! Do something with them!

How do you treat good ideas? By *acting* on them, that's how!

Alfred Moore

Many years ago, when the beautiful Union Railroad Station was built in Cincinnati, Ohio, spectacular mosaics were created on the plastered walls. They artfully depicted the crafts and industry of the city of Cincinnati.

As years went by, the building began to sag. When it was condemned, people were horrified. What would happen to the exquisite mosaics? Destroying them along with the building was unthinkable.

Yet, when the experts were consulted, they replied, "There is no way to save the mosaics when the building is destroyed."

Alfred Moore refused to accept that answer. He could not let the mosaics be destroyed. He decided that he would find a way. That decision was the key that unlocked his mind. He thought of one possible way the twenty-by-twenty foot panels could be moved.

He created a gigantic steel frame for each section of the wall. Then he put wire nets on the back side of the walls, and sprayed them with gunnite—the wet concrete that is used in swimming pools. Then, with a huge crane, he lifted the walls, transported them, and installed them in the new airport. They are there today!

When faced with a mountain,
I will not quit!
I will keep on striving
until I climb over, find a pass through,
tunnel underneath
—or simply stay
and turn the mountain
into a gold mine,
with God's help!

"*Now to Him who is able to do exceedingly abundantly above all that we ask or think, according to the power that works in us, to Him be glory. . . . Amen.*" EPHESIANS 3:20–21